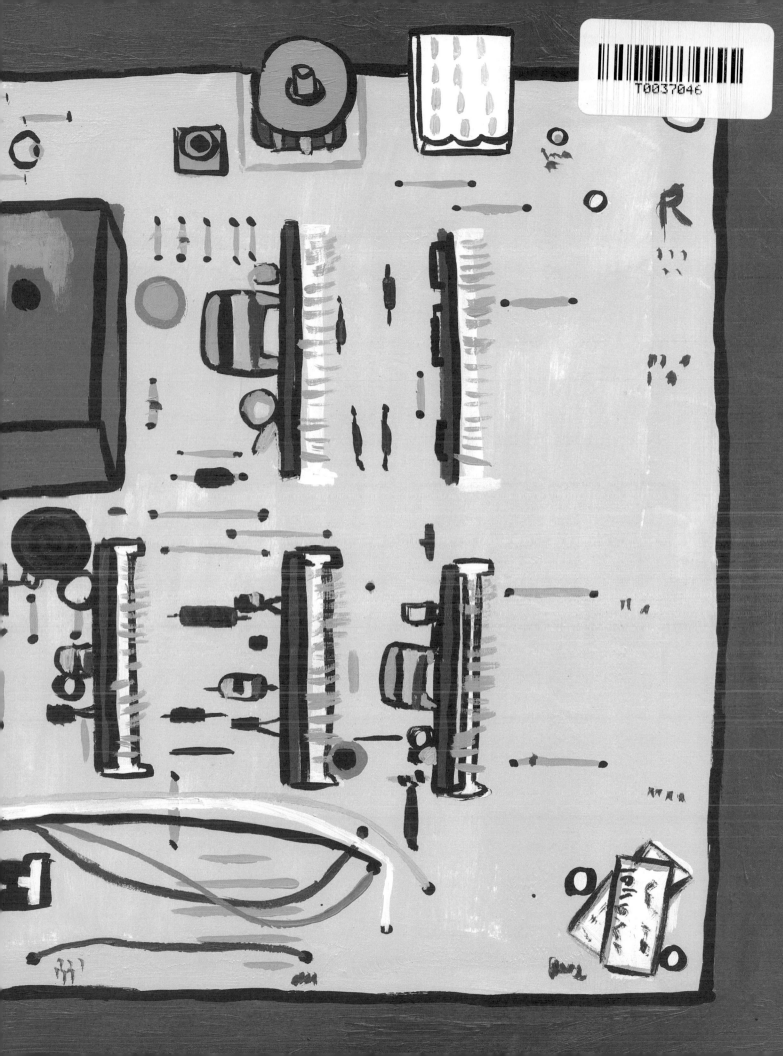

BLIPS
ON A SCREEN

How Ralph Baer Invented
TV Video Gaming and Launched
a Worldwide Obsession

WRITTEN BY
KATE HANNIGAN

ILLUSTRATED BY
ZACHARIAH OHORA

Alfred A. Knopf ❧ New York

For Gabriel Issa, who's made good use of this invention
—K.H.

For the two kids always playing video games in the living room
—Z.O.

THIS IS A BORZOI BOOK PUBLISHED BY ALFRED A. KNOPF

Text copyright © 2022 by Kate Hannigan
Jacket art and interior illustrations copyright © 2022 by Zachariah OHora

Family photos courtesy of the Ralph H. Baer Trust and the Baer family through the Ralph H. Baer Papers,
Archives Center, National Museum of American History, Smithsonian Institution.
The Brown Box image courtesy of the Division of Medicine and Science,
National Museum of American History, Smithsonian Institution.

Visit us on the Web! rhcbooks.com

Educators and librarians, for a variety of teaching tools, visit us at RHTeachersLibrarians.com

Library of Congress Cataloging-in-Publication Data
Names: Hannigan, Kate, author. | OHora, Zachariah, illustrator.
Title: Blips on a screen : how Ralph Baer invented TV video gaming and launched a worldwide obsession /
written by Kate Hannigan ; illustratedby Zachariah OHora. Description: First edition. | New York:
Alfred A. Knopf, an imprint of Random House Children's Books, [2022] | Includes bibliographical references. |
Audience: Ages 4–8. | Audience: Grades K–1. | Summary:
"A picture-book biography of Jewish refugee Ralph Baer, the pioneering inventor of home video gaming."—Provided by publisher.
Identifiers: LCCN 2021008883 | ISBN 978-0-593-30671-0 (hardcover) | ISBN 978-0-593-30672-7 (library binding) |
ISBN 978-0-593-30673-4 (ebook) Subjects: LCSH: Baer, Ralph H.—Juvenile literature. | Video game designers—United States—
Biography—Juvenile literature. | Inventors—United States—Biography—Juvenile literature. |
Video games—History—Juvenile literature. Classification: LCC GV1469.3.B33 H36 2022 | DDC 794.8092 [B]—dc23

The text of this book is set in 14.5-point Eames Century Modern.
The illustrations were created using acrylic paint on BFK Rives printmaking paper.
Book design by Nicole de las Heras

MANUFACTURED IN CHINA
April 2022
10 9 8 7 6 5 4 3 2
First Edition

Rudolf "Rolf" Baer loved games.
Money and food had grown scarce everywhere
after the Great Depression began in 1929.

Rolf looked for ways to make life a little more fun.

Chase, chess, handball, and kickball were good
distractions for his sister, Ilse, and their friends in his
German hometown.

When Rolf turned ten, Adolf Hitler and the Nazi Party were blaming Jews for Germany's problems. They kicked Jewish kids out of school.

Suddenly Rolf's classmates didn't want to play with him anymore.

Facing imprisonment and even death, the Baers fled Germany just weeks before the border closed. When they reached New York City in 1938, the children changed their names to the less German-sounding Ralph and Jane.

Sixteen now, Ralph had no more time for games. He took a job in a leather factory and, with an inventor's spirit, quickly found ways to make the machines run better.

On the subway to work one morning, Ralph noticed an advertisement.

He liked the idea of working with radios—people around the world tuned in every day to gasp over mystery shows, laugh with comedians, and worry over wartime news. He enrolled in radio-repair classes.

I chased all over New York City repairing radios. Did it all myself—pickups, repairs, deliveries.

After America joined World War II in 1941, Ralph used
his radio skills in the army.

But once he returned from England and France,
he looked to the future:

TELEVISION!

Veterans were coming home and buying houses. And television
sets brought newscasters and celebrities right into viewers' living
rooms! Within a few years, more than fifteen million households
owned one.

Ralph took a job designing televisions, but he found it boring to passively watch a screen. With their crisscrossing lines, he said, they "looked suspiciously like board games . . . so why not use them to play games?"

"You're already late," his bosses said. "No time for games."

For fifteen years, Ralph pushed the idea of TV gaming aside. Working at military electronics companies in New York and New Hampshire, he combined his radio and television knowledge with his army experience. Soon Ralph was inventing sonar systems for tracking submarines and "snooping equipment" for monitoring enemy radios.

But as he sipped his tea, drove his car, and tinkered in his basement workshop, Ralph couldn't stop thinking about making television more fun.

Ideas ping-ponged around in his head. Waiting for a bus one afternoon, Ralph sat down on a step, pulled out a pencil, and began to write them down. "What I had in mind was to develop a small 'game box' that would do neat things."

When Ralph returned to his office, he wrote up his notes. He knew it was important to **document** a great idea—not just to create a record of his invention, but to cement his place as the first person to come up with it!

He and a friend initialed each page and wrote the date:

September 1, 1966

As quickly as he could, Ralph began turning the lightbulb in his head into something real. He tested, tinkered, and tweaked his ideas until, finally . . .

a single blip appeared on
a screen.

Ralph stretched the spot tall,
collapsed it short,

swung it left

and right.

He called it

"TV GAME UNIT #1."

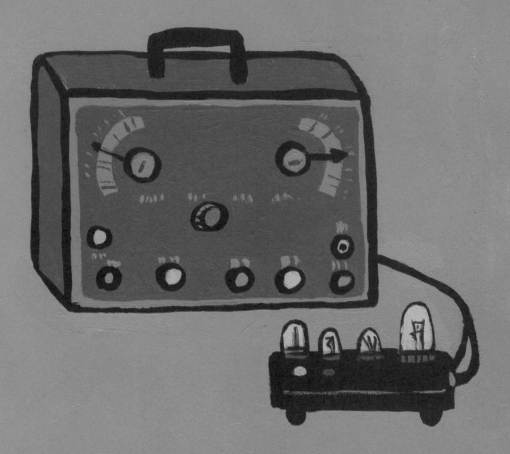

"This looks like it has potential," his boss said about
Ralph's **prototype**, or early model, "but it better do more
interesting things than this."

Ralph knew it could!

While his days were busy with top-secret research for the electronics company, Ralph locked himself in an office with another engineer, Bill Harrison, and worked deep into the night. Music blared behind the doors so nobody would know about their "classified project."

They taped a plastic overlay onto their TV screen to make the game look more engaging. It showed a picture of a bucket. Using two controllers pointed at one spot, Ralph and Bill pumped the line up or down, filling or draining the bucket. The calendar read May 15, 1967, marking the first two-person TV video game contest in history.

Ralph lost,
but he didn't mind!

Ralph added a second blip. Now his gaming system could
move a pair of squarish dots on a screen independently.

TWO-PLAYER CHASE GAMES
WERE BORN!

With help from engineer Bill Rusch, they introduced another spot. Now two players could interact with the third blip.

The minute that came along, we knew what the answer was: BALL GAMES.

"Are you still fooling around with that stuff?" asked his managers. Ralph certainly was.

Ralph worked long days and late nights—in the secret fifth-floor office he called the "little bitty room" and in his basement at home. "We played games downstairs in my lab, and the kids played them. They thought it was pretty neat."

He could barely contain his excitement for bringing games onto TV screens.

"I'd be driving home, and I'd stop at a red light . . . saying,

On January 15, 1968, Ralph applied for the first of many TV gaming **patents**, or legal protections, from the U.S. government. A patent ensures that inventors get not just the credit but also the money they're due from their inventions.

Ralph tested his ideas.
When they failed, he
tried again.

Together with his engineers, he strategized, simplified, streamlined.

By January 1969, Ralph was ready to show his jumble of wires, circuitry, and controllers to his bosses. Before the meeting, they decided their "TV Game Unit #7" needed spiffing up. Covering it in vinyl made to look like wood, they called this prototype the Brown Box.

Despite their stuffy suits and neckties, the bosses had fun with Ralph's games! But they were a little baffled.

Ralph did know. He would have to find another company to **implement**, or produce and sell, his invention. But how? And who? For the next year, he took the Brown Box to everyone he could find in the TV business.

But nobody had time for games.

Finally, one television company thought the Brown Box showed a hint of promise. They called it the *Skill-O-Vision*!

Later they renamed it the *Odyssey*.

As his invention rolled off assembly lines, Ralph
designed ways to make it even better. But nobody
listened. Ralph felt left out, ignored, forgotten.
"My objective was to help them, but help isn't
always appreciated."

Months passed, and Ralph began to have doubts.
Would anybody want to play? Was it all a waste of time?
Lying in a hospital bed after minor surgery, Ralph stared
at the walls and felt blue.

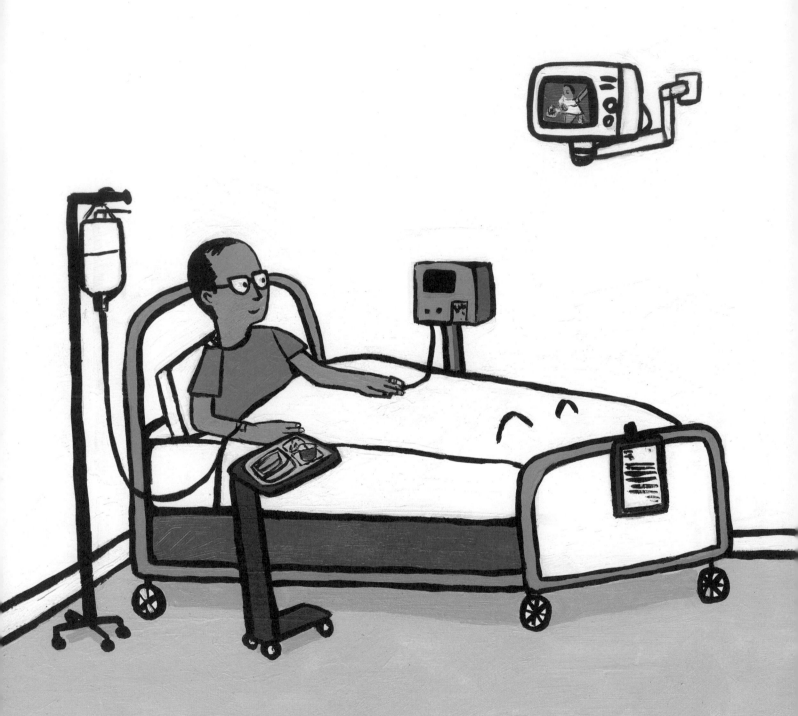

Suddenly his colleagues rushed into the room carrying an oversize check from the TV company. And on it was written a big number: $100,000!

The Odyssey was taking off!

For Ralph Baer—and for game lovers around the world—
life was about to become *a whole lot* more fun.

"FANTASTIC! BY FAR,
THE GAME OF THE CENTURY."
—user feedback, November 1972

QUESTIONS & ANSWERS

Who built the first video game and gaming system?

Ralph Baer did! When kids started playing the Odyssey in 1972, it was the world's first TV video gaming system, and the games on it were the world's first video games. Magnavox, the company that produced the Odyssey, sold over 330,000 units and launched scores of competitors.

Did it catch on?

You betcha! What started out as a few blips on a screen has grown into a worldwide industry and pastime—with the number of video gamers reaching into the billions. People young and old play video games for hours every day, watch other people play video games, and even become e-sports athletes.

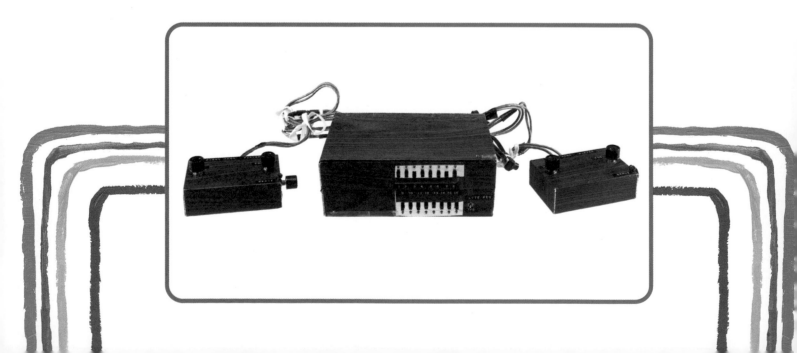

Was this Ralph's only invention?

No way! The Brown Box was just one of many exciting inventions Ralph pioneered. Over his lifetime, Ralph secured more than 150 U.S. and foreign patents.

What else did he make?

Aside from igniting the home video game craze, he developed lots of electronic toys and games. His most popular is *Simon,* a light-up game named for the children's game Simon Says, which hit stores in 1978 and is still produced today. A recordable talking doormat, recordable talking books, a talking speedometer for bikes, interactive talking toys, and stand-alone computer games are some of the examples of his work. Ralph's list of inventions runs long!

What made Ralph so special?

Sometimes it might seem as if inventors possess magical qualities that make their creations catch fire. But often it's just the right combination of timing, skill, and enthusiasm. For Ralph, his service in World War II helped him understand military technology, and his job building television sets gave him expertise with an exciting new medium. His self-motivation and big imagination put him further down the road to success. So as he worked at

his day job developing sonar tools to find enemy targets, it wasn't too different from building a *Fox and Hounds* video game of chase.

Did anyone pay attention to Ralph's invention?

Yes! While he didn't get rich off his video gaming invention—most of the licensing money went to his employer, Sanders Associates—Ralph received many honors over the years. The biggest was the National Medal of Technology from President George W. Bush in 2006. Four years later, he was inducted into the National Inventors Hall of Fame!

Did Ralph's children get to test out the games?

They did! Which makes Nancy, Mark, and James Baer the world's very first kid-gamers!

Did Ralph have advice for aspiring inventors?

Ralph's advice is simple: believe in your idea. "Follow your guts and instinct," he said later in life, "because you won't be happy if you don't do it."

How can I learn more?

Ralph's legacy as the inventor of the first TV video games and gaming system, which formed the bedrock for the modern video game industry, is preserved at the Smithsonian's National Museum of American History in Washington, D.C., and at the Strong Museum of Play in Rochester, New York. While exploring his re-created workshops and studying his Brown Box, documents, prototypes, and patents, maybe you'll find the inspiration to be like Ralph and develop the next great, world-changing invention!

"I'm first and foremost an inventor.
But what we created was indeed art."
—Ralph Baer

Inventors like Ralph live for the next brilliant idea, called a *Eureka!* moment. But protecting that great invention born in their brain—known as "intellectual property"—is crucial to inventors' survival. Otherwise, competitors can take the terrific notion and run with it, leaving the inventor unable to claim credit or to earn a living.

Ralph's journey to create the world's first TV video games and home gaming system demonstrates the four crucial steps every inventor must take when developing an idea into a product:

1. **Document**, or write it down
2. **Prototype**, or create a model
3. **Patent**, or file for protection
4. **Implement**, or produce and sell

If he'd neglected to do any of these things, recognition of Ralph's groundbreaking work and his title as "the Father of Video Games" might have gone to someone else. By applying for various TV gaming patents, Ralph and Sanders Associates secured exclusive rights to ball-and-paddle games that other developers would have to honor.

"Whatever you do," Ralph said, "sign it, date it, never, ever throw anything away. Keep every scrap of paper."

Inventors and inventions have always been important to advancement in any society. America's founders thought inventions were so essential to the country's progress, they wrote patent protections into the U.S. Constitution—to ensure that inventors like Ralph, and maybe even YOU, would take risks to create new things and move society forward.

"The Congress shall have power to . . . promote the progress of science and useful arts, by securing for limited times to authors and inventors the exclusive right to their respective writings and discoveries."

—Constitution of the United States, Article 1, Section 8, Paragraph 8

TIMELINE

March 8, 1922
Rudolf Heinrich Baer is born in Pirmasens, Germany, and raised in Cologne.

1927
First electronic television is invented.

1936
Forced to abandon school because he is Jewish.

August 1938
Flees Nazi Germany, via Holland, to New York City; changes name to Ralph.

1938, November 9–10
Kristallnacht—"the Night of Broken Glass"—when windows of Jewish-owned homes, shops, and synagogues are destroyed and families are terrorized by Nazis. Virtually no one was allowed to leave Germany after this point.

Young Ralph and his sister

1940
Graduates from National Radio Institute as radio service technician.

1941
Japanese military attacks Pearl Harbor in Hawaii, pulling U.S. into World War II.

1943
Receives U.S. citizenship, is drafted, serves three years in military intelligence for U.S. Army in England and France.

1949
Graduates with BS in television engineering from American Television Institute of Technology in Chicago.

Teenage Ralph, 1939

1949–56
Works in military electronics for various companies.

1953
Marries Dena Whinston; they have three children, James, Mark, and Nancy.

1955
Family leaves New York for Manchester, New Hampshire.

1956–90
Joins military electronics company Sanders Associates in Nashua, New Hampshire, and serves in variety of positions over decades, including engineer, manager, and consultant.

1958
Willy Higinbotham creates tennis game on oscilloscope for one-off public demonstration, foreshadowing later video games.

1962
Steve Russell invents *Spacewar!* to run on MIT supercomputer, considered first computer-based electronic game.

September 1, 1966
Documents his idea for creating interactive TV system, including gaming.

1966–68
Prototypes "TV Game Unit #1" through "#7" with engineers Bill Harrison and Bill Rusch.

May 15, 1967
First two-person TV video game contest. Ralph loses water-bucket game to Bill Harrison.

July 1970
Demonstrates "TV Game Unit #7," known as "the Brown Box," to key executives at Magnavox.

March 3, 1971
Files agreement with Magnavox allowing them to license the technology from both Ralph and his employer, Sanders Associates.

March 22, 1971
Files patent application for "Television Gaming and Training Apparatus," No. 3,728,480, first patent to cover concept of playing games on TV; was continuation for preliminary patent application No. 697,798, filed on January 15, 1968.

April 1972
Magnavox implements Odyssey TV gaming system, eventually selling over 330,000 units.

November 1972
Atari introduces arcade ping-pong video game *Pong* after attending Odyssey demonstration.

1974
Magnavox pursues legal action against Atari and other video game companies for patent infringement.

1975
Several companies introduce home video games.

June 8, 1976
Atari settles with Magnavox out of court and becomes a licensee.

1976–83
Second generation of home gaming consoles like Atari 2600, Mattel's Intellivision, and ColecoVision gain users. But they initially fail to beat popularity of arcade video games.

1977
Judge rules in favor of Magnavox in *Intellivision v. Magnavox*, which goes on to win more than $100 million in patent lawsuits and settlements over the years.

1978
Invents *Simon*, light-up sequencing game that is a hit with the public.

1980
Pac-Man arcade game appears, followed by *Ms. Pac-Man* two years later.

1981
Nintendo launches *Donkey Kong* arcade video game, featuring mustache-wearing character Jumpman, who later is called Mario.

1985
Nintendo Entertainment System (NES) is released, securing home video gaming's popularity; over the next two years, Nintendo sells over 60 million consoles.

2006
Receives National Medal of Technology from President George W. Bush, who calls Ralph "the Father of Video Games."

With President George W. Bush, 2006

2010
Inducted into the National Inventors Hall of Fame.

December 7, 2014
Ralph Baer passes away at midnight in Manchester, New Hampshire, at age 92. (While some accounts list his death as December 6, Ralph's family, the coroner, and his gravestone record it as December 7.)

July 2015
His lab is installed in the Smithsonian Institution's National Museum of American History, allowing the public to see firsthand the origins of TV gaming.

RESOURCES

Books

Baer, Ralph H. *Videogames: In the Beginning.* Springfield, NJ: Rolenta Press, 2005

Burnham, Van. *Supercade: A Visual History of the Videogame Age 1971–1984.* Cambridge, MA: MIT Press, 2001

Goldberg, Harold. *All Your Base Are Belong to Us: How Fifty Years of Videogames Conquered Pop Culture* New York: Three Rivers Press, 2011

Kent, Steven L. *The Ultimate History of Video Games: From Pong to Pokemon and Beyond.* New York: Three Rivers Press, 2001

Ponce de Leon, Charles L. *That's the Way It Is: A History of Television News in America.* Chicago: University of Chicago Press, 2015

Wyckoff, Edwin Brit. *The Guy Who Invented Home Video Games.* New York: Enslow Elementary, 2010

Periodicals & Documents

Constitution of the United States

The Gazette (Janesville, Wisconsin), October 9, 2000

The Progress-Index (Petersburg, Virginia), February 3, 1977

Ralph Baer: Seven Decades in Electronics, Video, and Games. Presented at the NHJES 2nd Annual Joint Engineering Societies Conference, Manchester, NH, October 9, 2008

The Salt Lake Tribune, November 7, 2011

The Sun (Lowell, Massachusetts), October 4, 1981

Smithsonian Magazine (online), "Remembering the 'Father of Video Games,' Innovator Ralph Baer." December 8, 2014

smithsonianmag.com/smithsonian-institution/remembering-innovator-ralph-baer-father-video -games-180953555/

Websites & Museums

Computer History Museum: "Oral History of Ralph Baer," interviewed by Gardner Hendrie, October 12–November 27, 2006, Manchester, New Hampshire. archive.computerhistory.org/resources/text/ Oral_History/Baer_Ralph_1/Baer_Ralph_1and2.2006.102657972_final.pdf

Inventors Eye, United States Patent and Trademark Office's bimonthly magazine, "Simon Says: Invent," April 2010. uspto.gov/custom-page/spark

Ralph H. Baer Trust at RalphBaer.com. ralphbaer.com/biography.htm

Retro Gamer, "The Legacy of Ralph," by Retro Gamer Team, December 8, 2014. retrogamer.net/profiles/ developer/the-legacy-of-ralph-baer/

Smithsonian Institution National Museum of American History. americanhistory.si.edu/collections/ object-groups/the-father-of-the-video-game-the-ralph-baer-prototypes-and-electronic-games

Strong National Museum of Play. museumofplay.org/about/icheg/video-game-history/timeline

United States Patent and Trademark Office. uspto.gov/kids/index.html

ACKNOWLEDGMENTS

Grateful thanks to Mark W. Baer, son of Ralph Baer and trustee of the Ralph H. Baer Trust; and Dr. Arthur Molella, founding director of the Lemelson Center for the Study of Invention and Innovation at the Smithsonian's National Museum of American History in Washington, D.C.

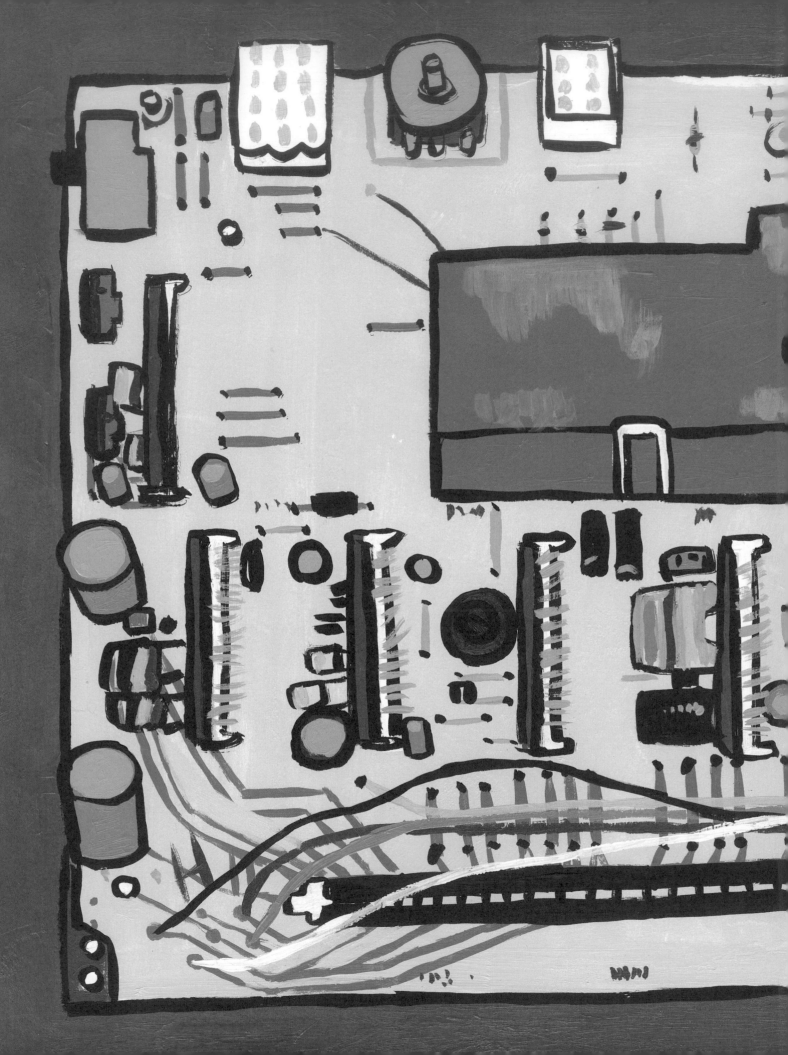